I0753668

Mystic Siren

Woman's Voice in the Balance of Creation

Vanessa Paloma

Mystic Siren:

Woman's Voice in the Balance of Creation

Artwork and Design by Gloria Abella Ballen

Gaon Books

Gaon Books
An imprint of
World Arts Press
Santa Fe, New Mexico
www.gaonbooks.com

Library of Congress Control Number: 2007932867

Paloma, Vanessa
Mystic Siren: Woman's Voice in the Balance of Creation/
Vanessa Paloma
ISBN: 978-0-9777514-5-7 pb

1. Religion 2. Judaism 3. Kabbalah & mysticism 4. Women's Studies 5. Sephardic Judaism 6. Ladino 7. Music

British Cataloging-in-Publication data for this book is available from the British Library.

Manufactured in the United States of America

Dedicated to

Aisha Evita
Crystal Leigh
Emilio
Izak León
Lucía
Lukas Uriel
Natasha Sumaya
Nina Tova
&
Ayala Hanah Aisha

Hoping that when you grow up you will express yourselves fully and beautifully and sing the song of your deepest essence.

Contents

Sirens and Women

Las Sirenas/The Sirens

Teachings

Poetic Reflections

Concluding

Acknowledgements

I am first of all grateful to the Creator (*Ribbono shel Olam*) for the opportunities and abilities that have led me to develop the thoughts expressed here.

Thanks to Rabbi Yehoshua Levin Landau for the many hours of Torah in the Rashash's study in the Old City while I lived in Jerusalem. His concern for my spiritual development and learning has had a long lasting effect. My learning with Rabbi Yitzhak Ginsburgh during his visits to Los Angeles helped me forge a completely new relationship to the secrets in Judaism. Rabbi Elchonon Tauber has been a great support as my Rav; his constant encouragement on the importance of a direct, daily and personal connection to the Creator through meditation (*hitbodedut*) has been invaluable to my own practice.

Thanks to Avivah Zornberg, who during my first weeks in Jerusalem assured me that I could be a singer and delve into Orthodox practice. She had just given a riveting class on the song of Miriam and the power of a woman's voice and took my concern about the seeming incompatibility of Orthodoxy as a professional singer very seriously. It was my honor to be a weekly *hevruta* (study partner) with Tamar Frankiel for some years and I cherish the learning we still do together. Her knowledge on such a wide range of topics and inquisitive intellect is a real inspiration. Thanks to Jorge Neves for taking me to the Palácio das Sereias in Porto. Thanks to him and Alfândega Filmes for the photographs of the Palácio.

I am grateful to The Center for Jewish Culture and Creativity for the years I worked very closely with them and the 2000 residency at Herzliya's Mishkan Omanim. Thanks to Alvaro Pérez Betancourt who has believed in my work and vision and has encouraged me to develop as a performer, teacher, writer and artist.

I am immensely grateful to my parents, Ron and Gloria, for their meaningful presence, and to my Mother for being the collaborating artist and designer on this volume. I am fortunate to have them as mentors, colleagues and friends; they are wonderful and as I get older I appreciate them and the rich upbringing they gave me even more.

Lastly, to Shulamith, Maimon and Ayala Chocron–our shared conversations, Shabbatot, holidays, songs and struggles make my life so much richer. Ayala planted the first seed for this book.

Vanessa Paloma
Los Angeles
Tu B'Av 5767/July 29, 2007

Foreword

The voices of Jewish women are coming forward in our times – not only the political voices participating in the public sphere, or the voices of social concern defending women from abuse, but also spiritual voices, speaking of women's profound insights, mystical experiences, and yearnings for the touch of the divine. Moreover, these voices are not only from contemporary life but also from deep within our history, even within song lyrics and mythology. In this collection, Vanessa Paloma gives life to some of these voices.

To grasp the deeper meaning, we have to understand Serena, the siren. The root of the Greek word means 'to bind or attach, but it has come to refer almost exclusively to the beautiful women with melodious voices who promise men wisdom, but are dangerous and even deadly. The idea is not confined to Greek mythology. We find a reworking of the same motifs in a story from Rabbi Nachman of Breslov, entitled "The King and the Emperor." There, the heroine of the story (the daughter of the emperor) and her companions, eleven daughters of nobles, are the dangerous women. In one episode, the twelve noblewomen convince twelve pirates to marry them – that is, to 'bind or attach' themselves – and, after putting them to sleep with a select wine at the wedding celebration, slit their husbands' throats. These women are represented as masters of all kinds of music and instruments, and symbolically represent the temple incense, which gives mystical wisdom.

While psychoanalytical approaches might regard these stories as representing men's fear of women, and particularly of the ties of marriage, from a Jewish perspective we can see the matter differently. Binding (as in the Akedat Yitzchak, the binding of Isaac) alludes to self-sacrifice, and attachment, devekut, in modern spiritual literature of the Hasidim requires the death, i.e. the nullification, of the ego. The sirens represent the possibility of opening to the Divine in the most profound ways, but also require the death of the hero. The heroic ego is as far as man can go by himself; but when he binds himself to woman, something much greater can emerge.

Until our times, this process has operated only on the unconscious level. Jewish tradition has explicitly upheld the view that a man can be complete only in marriage to a woman, but the inner dynamic of the relationship has remained hidden from view, except among the mystics. Now we are coming into an era when both men and women can accept this more fully – men to accept their spiritual dependence on women, and women to accept their awesome responsibility.

All of us will change as this process develops. It is so different from what conscious history has told us that we may not want to admit it at first. But when we allow ourselves to be open, in a gentle and compassionate way, to one another, we will all – men and women alike – emerge the better for it. We can be grateful for the work of Vanessa Paloma for helping the Flower of the Siren to open more and more fully.

Tamar Frankiel, Ph.D.
Author of *The Voice of Sarah* and *The Gift of Kabbalah*
Dean of Students and Professor of Comparative Religion,
Academy for Jewish Religion, California

Mystic Siren:

Woman's Voice in the Balance of Creation

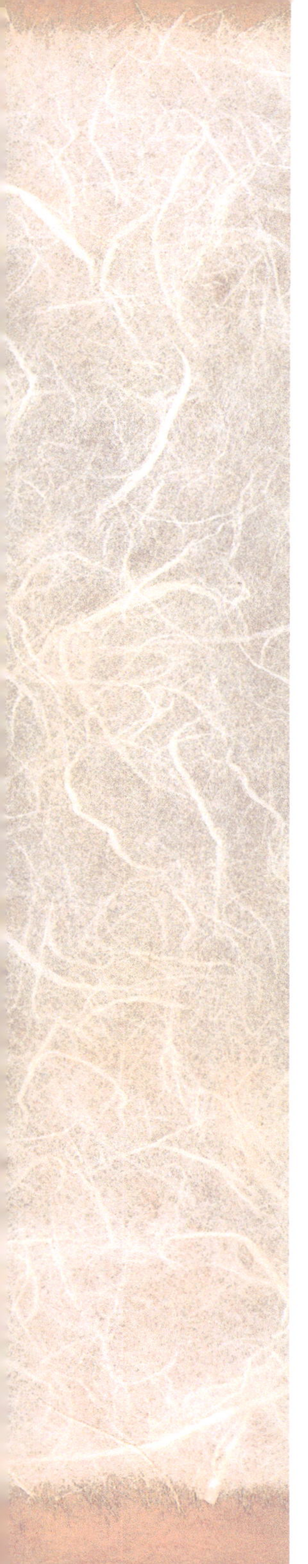

Sirens and Women: An Introduction

One night, the five-year-old daughter of a good friend came to sleep over because her parents were going out, and the baby-sitter didn't show. As I was putting her to bed, she asked me for a story. I have put her to bed several times since she was a baby, and I always make up a story or a song for her, the way my own father did with me when I was her age.

The only thing I could think of was this beautiful building "Palácio Das Sereias" in Porto, Portugal. Two giant sirens flank this beautiful house and it overlooks the Douro River on the site of the medieval Jewish quarter. I was there during the Passover intermediate days (*Chol HaMoed*) 5767/2007. Filmmaker Jorge Neves from Alfândega-Filmes, one of the founders of *Ladina* (a non-profit society dedicated to rescuing the memory and culture of the Portuguese Jewish people) and an active member of the Jewish community in Porto brought me to this unusual house, which is now a home for aging nuns.

There was something magical that morning when we stood outside of the Siren's Palace during Pesaj in Portugal, it was a sunny day with a crisp breeze overlooking the beautiful river. I could feel the history of Porto's rich Jewish heritage coming back to life through the recapturing of memories, places and noteworthy figures.

That night as I told Ayala the story that came to mind, her eyes

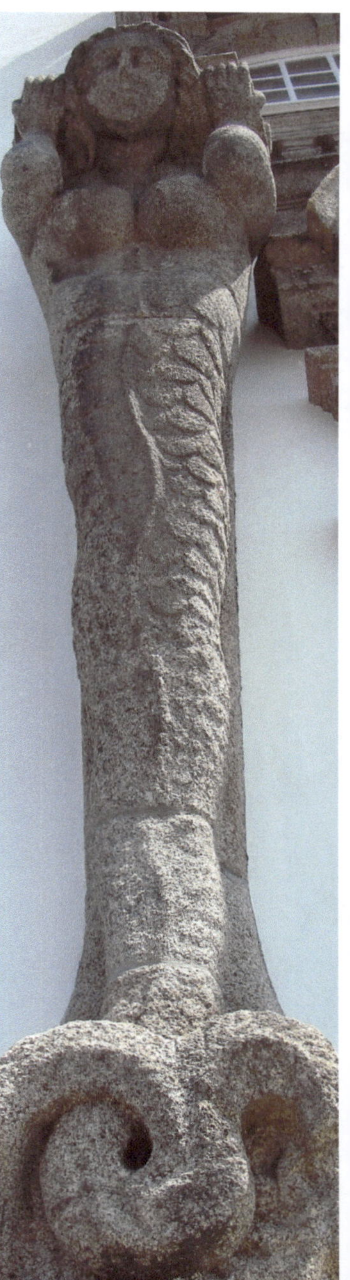

were growing wider and wider. She named the fisherman and the girl. She was most definitely NOT falling asleep! But by the end, she said, you should really write this down so that other people can hear it. This is a great story.

In thinking about it later, I realized that the Palácio was only the starting point that brought out other elements I have been thinking about and dealing with in my work. Through this fable, they came together in an unconscious manner. I am a professional singer specializing in Sephardic music, and the first connection comes through my group's name, *Flor de Serena* or Siren's Flower, a name chosen years ago.

Another connection is the title of one of the most famous Ladino songs, *La Serena*, which talks about a young woman living in a tower by the ocean. The seeker/sailor comes to her and begs to stay with her, so she isn't cursed by sleeping alone.

I was inspired to search out the meaning of Siren.

Sirens have a beguiling reputation with fearful overtones. As mythical beings, they lure sailors with their beautiful singing from their perches on rocks jutting out of the ocean. As the ships approach, they are dashed on the rocks and lost. With tragedy the siren is left alone, and the sailor dies because of his lack of caution.

Sirens were originally conceived in Greek mythology as women with a bird's body, but later the fish-woman imagery of the mermaid became more common. This combination of bird-fish-human is very significant because it brings together sky, sea and land. This is a creature that has dominion of all the realms where there is life on our planet.

Sirens are also described as women who are seductive, tempting, dangerous or harmful. They symbolize the danger of woman's sexuality and the irresistible nature of some women over men. A Siren's song refers to a call that is difficult to resist but that will lead to a bad result if heeded.

In his *Notebooks* Leonardo da Vinci wrote the following on the siren:

> *The siren sings so sweetly as to lull the mariners to sleep; then she climbs upon the ships and kills the sleeping mariners.*

In 1917, Franz Kafka wrote in *The Silence of the Sirens*:

> *Now the Sirens have a still more fatal weapon than their song, namely their silence. And though admittedly such a thing never happened, it is still conceivable that someone might possibly have escaped from their singing; but from their silence certainly never.*

Clearly we are faced with a deep fear of woman's expression and sensuality. This myth gives us an insight into an element that is present in the subconscious of our society. Woman's song and beauty equal man's destruction and death.

It seems to be related to the Jewish law (*Halacha*) of *Kol Isha*. This law is one that I wrestle with since I am an observant woman who is also a professional singer. *Kol Isha* (woman's voice) says that a man may not listen to a woman solo singing, unless it is his wife, daughter, mother or sister. Singing is considered to reveal a very intimate part of the person. Hearing a woman's singing may sexually arouse or entice a man, so he must refrain from listening.

The consequence of this underlying subconscious theme is that many women are afraid to develop their expressive capacities because they fear appearing to be enticing, alluring, beguiling and ultimately dangerous. My question is can we turn this around? How can we take the sensuous power of woman to be a gift and not something to fear? Why has this most powerful aspect of woman been demonized and taken to be a negative trait?

The beauty of a femininity is connected to new life, passion and love. It can be seen as a dangerous allure, or a mysterious and powerful aspect of the polarity between masculine and feminine energies. Women's acknowledgement of the power in their voice and their use of it in a meaningful way can be healing for them and the men who hear them.

The story of the *sereias* came to me in the last days of the *Omer*, the forty-seventh day. It was the evening of May 19, 2007. When I went to the *Omer* calendar I discovered it was the night of *Hod she'beMalchut* (i.e. dignity in sovereignty). I decided to do an Internet search on teachings on the meaning of that specific day. On *www.ritualwell.org,* Jill Hammer describes the energy of *Hod she'beMalchut* as:

> *When Esther stands in the throne room before the king, she is wearing royal robes–literally, she is wearing malkhut. Though Esther is not born a queen, she achieves dignity through her willingness to take dramatic action to save her people. She has not chosen her position of power, but she knows that her position must be used for the benefit of others. She is an exemplar of Hod she'bemalkhut–the acceptance of power. We are most like her when we ask ourselves how we can use our own power and privilege to serve God and our fellow beings.*

I was amazed. Without being aware of it, the story that came to me as I was trying to put little Ayala to sleep, was exactly connecting to the *Omer* we had just counted when the sun had gone down. And so much of my work deals with the importance of women accepting their power, using their voice and taking dramatic action for our people.

In this volume I put together a series of pieces that will lead the reader to delve inside and find their own voice, their own power and their own essence. It is not an easy journey, at times it is very lonely and there are many setbacks. But, the sweetness of those moments when one's voice blends with the voice of creation are what give strength and propel the next level on the journey.

Las Serenas

The Sirens

Sirens are a symbol of the potential for both beauty and destruction that each of us carries inside. Use these stories to uncover the infinity of your own inner resources.

Palacio das SereiaS

There was a bustling city that spread across both the banks of a great river. It had beautiful hills and winding alleyways of mysterious passages leading from one world to another. From one side of the river you could look across and see the lights blinking at night on the other side, and in the daytime you could see the beautiful façades of the houses in yellow, blue and white.

At the top of one of these hills was a stunning house. It was perched high on a hill so that you could look down on the boats floating along the river, and you could also see out to the place where the river and the ocean waters met in the kiss of the salty and sweet waters. This was an imposing, tall three-story house painted a gleaming white, and it had a huge front door flanked by two gigantic sirens (mermaids) carved in stone.

A girl named Mia lived in this house, and she would walk in and out through the siren door every day on her way to school. One day when she was coming home, the sirens called her name "Mia" just as she started to enter the door. She was shocked that the statues spoke and asked them how they knew her name. They said that they knew not only hers but her grandmother's and great-grandmother's as well. There was a secret they had to tell her. They had been waiting until she was old enough to understand and to carry out a special responsibility. She had no idea what they were talking about, but it sounded so interesting that she asked what the secret was. They told her they would only tell her the secret if she were going to try to complete the task that they were asking her to do. So, she thought for a couple of minutes and agreed that she would try her best to fulfill her mission.

The Sirens told Mia that there was a secret passageway somewhere in the house and her task was to find it. Then she had to enter it and find the next step. She agreed and as soon as she went inside she started looking for a passageway in all the different rooms. She looked in her closet, in her mother's closet, in the bathroom, in the cellar and in the kitchen. Finally, when she looked under the kitchen sink she noticed a panel of wood on the back wall and as she pulled it off, she saw a whole passageway with descending stairs. Mia squirmed her way into the passageway which was tight at first, and then discovered how it became a larger and larger hallway with a high vaulted ceiling. At the end of the hallway a door opened to a small room, and inside Mia found a letter addressed to her, and it said that she was the chosen one to become an important leader of her people. But, first, she had to find a jeweled chest at the bottom of the sea with help of a fisherman called Danny. Inside the letter was a golden key.

When she came back into the house from the passageway, it was time for dinner. She hid the key and letter and joined her family in the dining room. She really wanted to tell the Sirens of her success, but now she would have to wait until the next morning. That night Mia had amazing dreams about swimming in the ocean with the Sirens. They were speaking to her underwater about all sorts of wonderful secret things.

Mia awoke at dawn, and she went out first thing to tell the Sirens what had happened. They were thrilled to hear her story about finding the passageway, the golden key, and the letter telling her what to do to uncover her special gifts.

Mia didn't know where to find Danny the fisherman, and she asked the Sirens where to start looking for him. They told her to go to the fish market down by the river and ask for Danny and then everything would be clear.

After school Mia went straight to the fish market with the key and the letter buried deep in her book bag. The fishmongers were arranged in long hallways on a small incline with all their fresh fish laid out on ice in front of them inside hand-made wicker baskets. Some had tiled counters with fish lined up and others were cleaning and boning the fish for customers. Water was running down the incline as fishmongers cleaned the fish and their counters. On all sides people were shouting prices and all sorts of fish names. Mia had never been here, and it was so interesting and full of action! She started asking people where she could find Danny the fisherman and after only asking three people someone pointed her in the right direction.

When Mia walked up to Danny, she noticed that his eyes were very gentle, and he seemed like he was beyond time. She couldn't really figure out how old he was, he was one of those ageless people. He was wearing baggy pants and a loose cotton shirt. Before she could speak, he looked right at her and said, "Wait here until I'm finished here, and then we'll go."

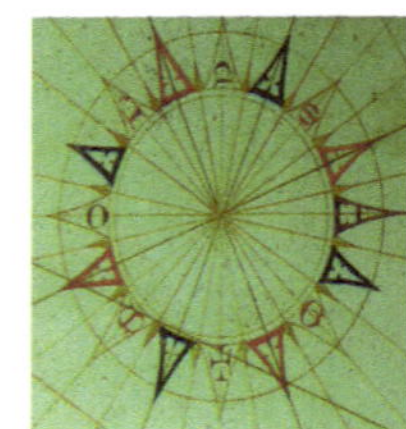

Mia sat down next to Danny's fish stand and watched all that was happening around her. About thirty minutes later Danny turned to her and said, "Ok, let's go."

They walked down toward the river and the docks where the boats wait patiently for their masters until they can float out joyously into the middle of the river and if they're lucky, out to the ocean itself. Danny was easy going, and he told Mia that he knew her mother and grandmother very well. Mia wondered if he had ever heard the Sirens speaking.

Danny said to Mia, "I know that you have a special task to complete. Your grandmother told me many years ago that you would come to look for me some day. Once you came, your destiny would start to unfold and my part in the puzzle is to take you out on my boat to a place you will indicate. If you are ready for your task, you will know how to pick the right spot." Now all of a sudden Mia got nervous. What if she picked the wrong spot? What would happen then? But then she looked at Danny, and his serene eyes calmed her down. She realized that she would know the right spot when they arrived to it.

Danny steered the boat into the center of the river, as they moved slowly toward the ocean. Mia felt a great sense of peace hearing the waves lap on the side of the boat. After sailing for a bit, she suddenly asked Danny to stop. She knew they had arrived. They were exactly at the point of confluence between the river and the ocean. Mia started to pray and asked to be ready to receive the message that the Sirens had sent her to discover. Danny dropped the anchor and waited to see what would happen. They waited, and they waited. The sun was hiding behind the clouds, it was one of those days with a lot of light but no sun. It was a gray whitish kind of day.

After some time had passed, Mia was starting to have the feeling that nothing was going to happen, but everything changed quickly. Both felt a lurch on the anchor line, and they started to reel it up. It was heavy and came from deep waters. When they pulled it to the surface, she gasped to see a long lost chest covered in barnacles. They wrestled it into the boat, and she pulled the key out of her bag and shaking with excitement put it in the keyhole and gave a turn. At first nothing happened, so she turned harder, still nothing. Then, with a grimace and all of the force she could muster, she gave another mighty turn on the key, and she heard a slow grinding, rusty noise in the lock. The latch fell open.

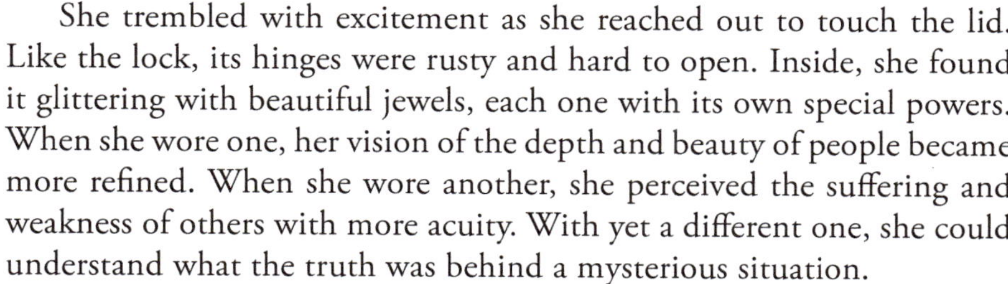

She trembled with excitement as she reached out to touch the lid. Like the lock, its hinges were rusty and hard to open. Inside, she found it glittering with beautiful jewels, each one with its own special powers. When she wore one, her vision of the depth and beauty of people became more refined. When she wore another, she perceived the suffering and weakness of others with more acuity. With yet a different one, she could understand what the truth was behind a mysterious situation.

But the only reason the jewels had this effect was because Mia was the person that was supposed to wear them. She knew how to use these jewels to help her people live a happier and more fulfilling life. She was the heiress of this tradition that had been locked away for many years waiting for her to be ready to accept her position and responsibility.

Danny took her back to the shore, and Mia gave him a special gift from the treasure chest.

Even though he did not want to accept anything, for him it was enough to have been the courier for this exceptional moment in the history of their city. Mia said that she wanted him to accept it, so he and his family could live an easier life. He could sell the jewel (which wasn't one of the ones with special qualities) and buy a house overlooking the river.

Mia went home and told the Sirens about Danny, the jewels and her experience unlocking the secret of her destiny. They were happy and proud of her courage to make the discovery, which would allow her to help so many others.

Word started spreading that finally the tradition of the visionary woman had been restored to their city. People would line up to go into the *Palácio Das Sereias* to see Mia. Each was touched by her great wisdom and inner peace. People that felt lost started to find their way. Everyone was inspired by this young girl's handle on the deepest truths of life and the whole city was restored to the same glory it had enjoyed during previous generations. People did not feel like they had to control or manipulate others. Difficult situations were handled with compassion and understanding. People started to open their hearts and minds to one another. Mia continued helping and being a healer for her people, she grew up, got married and had a wonderful husband. They had many children who ran through the yards and played games of mystery and fantasy, always knowing that their mother had been a girl who followed her dreams and had the courage to take risks that led to her greatness.

On the Power of Being Yourself

Once upon a time a baby girl was born to a man who came from the world of the earth and a woman who came from the world of the skies. They wandered the earth in search of family, happiness and their dreams. For the baby, who had become a child by now, it was a test to live time and time again in a new place, making new friends, learning a new language and a new culture. She always made friends and had the knack of easily learning to live in the place. They lived in the mountains surrounded by loving family and then in the tundra surrounded by snow, on an island surrounded by sea and mango trees, then in the mountains again. The girl started to sing and make music. Books were her best friends and her life was composed of having fun expressing herself in different ways.

One day the man and the woman decided to go to the land of the earth, and the girl, who was grown-up by now, did not want to go. In the beginning, she stayed, but later she went to join them in the land of the earth. She suffered a lot. She couldn't learn the tricks there and couldn't understand the people. Off she went to school where she found people that were more like her, and then she moved to the city of light.

Here in this new city she felt very lonely and lost, and she found that in her loneliness her family memories started taking over her life. She was fascinated by past traditions that had almost died but came flooding back, filling her soul with hope.

I wrote this piece during the first days of the second Intifada in September of 2000 in Israel, while in residence at Mishkan Omanim in Herzliya. There were helicopters flying overhead and flares were visible from our window.

With this fascination growing in her, she traveled to the land of dreams and learned a deep wisdom opening the door for her to express the unique gifts that defined who *she* was as a soul in the world.

Then she came back to the city of light where she splashed into the city with the expression of her self–not the one she had tried to learn in so many different places. She had a voice that grew from within her and started coming out more and more. This voice expressed all the voices that had been quiet for so many years, for generations.

The voice came and she sang of light and dreams and earth and sky and tundra and mountains and sea and all was ONE.

TeachingS

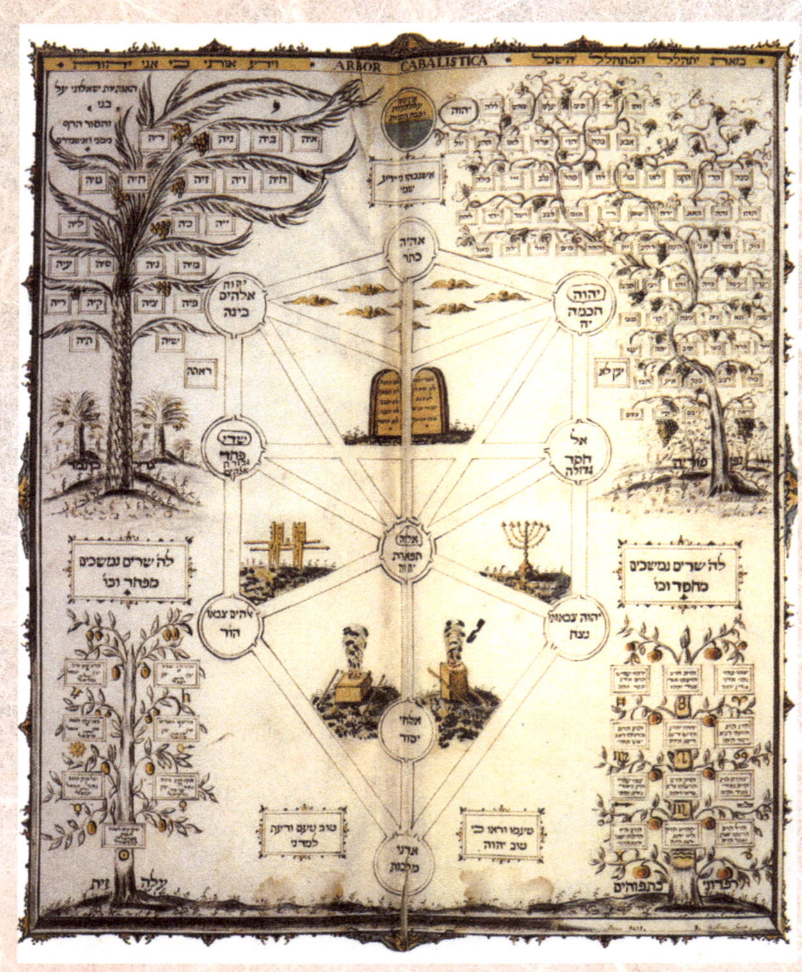

These teachings inspired by the Kabbalah of Rabbi Yitzhak Ginsburgh and Rabbi Moshe Cordovero can become daily exercises that will help you deepen your sensitivity towards yourself.

For more detailed information on Kabbalah, additional readings are suggested in the back of the book.

Life is A Song

Every life is a song. Every person has their own song, which is composed in their actions, thoughts, feelings, and way in the world. We spend our life trying to discover our own true personal song.

That is why for some people life is an easy and open field even with troubles along the way, nothing is too overwhelming to overcome. For others, life is constantly troubling and every situation becomes a difficult obstacle course. The people who are in harmony with their life song are "going with the melody flow" so to speak. They are living in accordance with their song. The others, who are constantly experiencing difficulty and perceiving every situation as an obstacle or burden are not living true to their song and that dissonance presents itself as a constant barrage of problems. The dissonance tries to make itself known, in this way the person can awaken from their dissonant lifestyle.

How do we know if we are living true to our song? Have you ever experienced those moments where everything seems to be working out with almost no effort? Where doors just seem to open up to you? These are moments when we are in harmony with our song. On the other hand, when everything seems to be going the wrong way and we are struggling with things that should be simple, our song is telling us that we are not living in harmony. Somehow we are distant from the ideal vibrations with which our soul connects.

Of course, some people's lives are fraught with more challenges than others. If you are living your song, even though life throws difficulties your way, you have the resources to deal with it. When we are not living our song, the challenges of life can feel much more burdensome.

The most difficult part of this process is learning to fine tune our inner ear to understand what our song actually is. It takes a lot of listening and a lot of standing up for who we are and not who we think we are or who we would like to be; but who we actually are in our deepest essential point.

In each individual process of fine tuning, there is the active process that takes place by standing up for our deepest wishes and visions of ourselves and our life. However, there is a passive process as well. Allowing the conscious ego-self to go dormant while a more super conscious self emerges from the background. This super conscious self knows the song but emerges only occasionally and gives us encoded hints. Our ears need to be open enough to hear the hints that will lead us slowly through years of refinement towards the fullest version of the song.

Just as Rebbe Nahman's teaching on song elucidates that each action is a note in a song that we are constantly creating—this song becomes deeper, more harmonized and complex throughout the ups and downs of life.

Dissonance

Have you ever heard a melody without moments of dissonance? It is very boring. A melody without moments of tension is bland and formless. Melodic, rhythmic or harmonic tension underline the moments of resolution marking them with more strength.

This is the purpose of problems. During the course of a melody there are moments of tension and release, the more exacerbated the tension, the release becomes more pleasing to the ear. The same is with problems in life. The more difficult the problem, the more complex the path of its resolutions will be, and finally when the solution comes, the degree of satisfaction is greater than what would have been before the problem even arose.

Humans derive great pleasure from resolution of problems. Once there are no problems people forget how good they actually have it. Think of a country before a great war. People are complaining about small annoyances in their daily life. Most have forgotten to appreciate the great myriad of blessings they have every day. A country after a great war that has finally come to peace after many years of pain, death and poverty is grateful for the gift of life and hope for the future. Even the simplest of pleasures bring a great satisfaction to even the most fortunate person.

This is why we need dissonance in music and in life. It is what brings the sweet moments their true sweetness. Through difficulties we appreciate the quality and quantity of our many blessings. We then are able to open our eyes to what we have been taking for granted.

Dissonance is the jolt that brings us to remember how great resolution is.

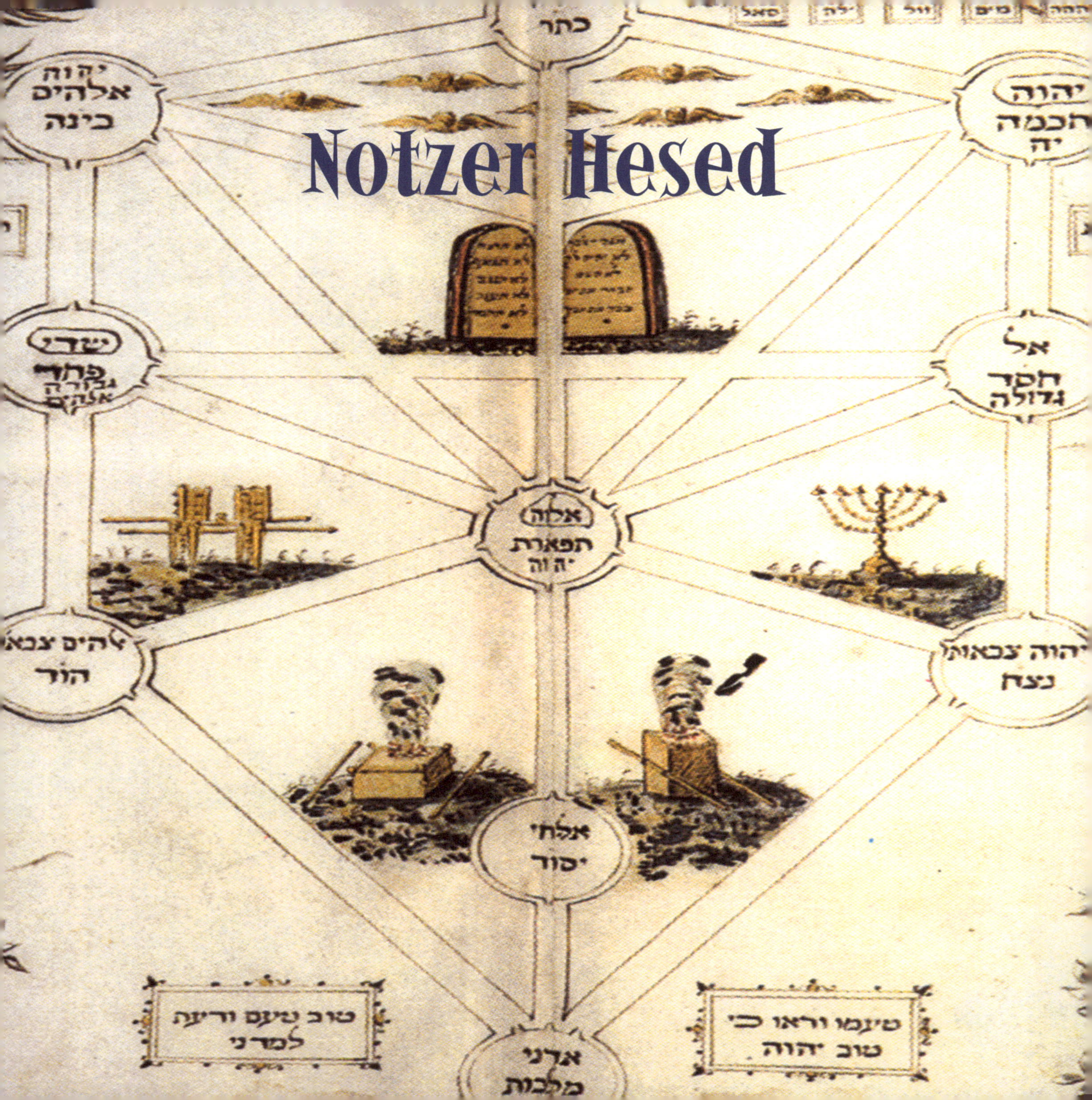

Notzer Hesed
כתר
יהוה
אלהים
בינה
יהוה
חכמה
יה
שדי
פחד
גבורה
אלהים
אל
חסד
גדולה
אלוה
תפארת
יהוה
להים צבא
הוד
יהוה צבאות
נצח
אלחי
יסוד
טוב טעם ודעת
למדני
טעמו וראו כי
טוב יהוה
אדני
מלכות

An Exercise on Drawing Out Hashem's Kindness

When reading *Tomer Devorah* (*The Palm Tree of Deborah*) I was struck in a profound and moving way when I realized the extent of Hashem's *hesed* (kindness) for us. It is difficult for us to understand the depth and level of love and bestowal of blessings from the higher world that we are constantly receiving. If we were really truly conscious of it, we would feel like what we have is enough! We would realize that our deeds will never measure up to the amount of sweetness that is in our life and how even with this, Hashem wants to continue showering us with blessings that are really just hovering over our head so to speak. However, with our unrectified speech, thoughts and deeds we have created blemishes in our *tsinorot* (conduits) which make it more difficult to receive Divine blessing. Even with these blemishes, small or large, Hashem still manages to shower us with blessings above and beyond our understanding. Can you only imagine what it would be like if our *tsinorot* were more clear?!

Hashem is *Notzer Hesed*, preserver of kindness. This is the fourth attribute of the thirteen attributes of G-d. The word *Notzer* is a permutation of *Tzinor* (conduit). It is through *tzinorot* that we as the *Kli* (vessel) are able to receive Hashem's blessings.

Rabbi Yitzhak Ginsburgh teaches on the issue of hair (which as is known, is hollow) as a conduit. It leads to the vessel which is the hole or pore out of which the hair grows. Each "hole" or pore is the *yud* of Hashem's ineffable name, while the hair is the *vav* of Hashem's name. The function of the *vav* of Hashem's name is to draw out blessings from the world beyond into this world.

Hashem is longing for us to clear out our *tzinorot*, so we can be more clear recipients of blessing. When we perfect ourselves, Hashem is moved and thrilled figuratively more deeply than we could ever understand. It is only in a state of further "clearing" that we can achieve our potential and truly do what our task is in this life. The more we are perfected, the more we do G-d's work and help to bring the final rectification of the whole world.

The exercise of clearing out our *tzinor* to facilitate Hashem's attribute of *Notzer Hesed* consists in using our breath, our mind and our voice. To breathe in is likened to the vav of Hashem's name that draws in blessing and life force in. As we breath in, picturing the *vav*, we then hold the breath into our body, the vessel. This stage is the *vav* into the *yud*. You might then ask where are the two missing *heis*? The higher *hei* is your thoughts, and the lower *hei* is your speech. Meditate on this and sing a *niggun* (a wordless melody) with the intention of rectifying your speech and your thoughts. It is through speech (*malchut*-sovereignty) that we create and destroy in this world. May we all merit to only create vessels for beauty and revealed blessings.

אלהים
בינה
יהוה
חכמה
יה

Poetic Reflections

Through poetry we explore the mystical interpretations of life and Kabbalah itself. In this section my personal poetry gives the opportunity to walk the labyrinth of words to discover the meanings that may lie within.

The lyrics of the classic Ladino song, *La Serena,* are given a midrashic interpretation to explore the depth of meanings that such a song contains. Like much of Ladino music, this was sung predominantly by women, and it reflects the longing for the presence of her love. Is it the earthly love or the Divine One, or both?

I Am a Vessel

Ribbono shel Olam, I know I am a vessel for You and Your music, light, and teachings to come into this world,
Allow me to be like a polished glass that lets all Your light through
Allow me to be like a diamond bouncing Your light beyond all limitations
Allow me to be like a riverbed,
facilitating the unimpeded flow of the water of Your Torah to irrigate our lives, our souls and our world.

Dio Alto y Bendicho, have mercy and compassion on the Jewish people
Bring Your fire back to those who relate to You in a tired way out of habit
Bring your fire back to those who feel they have never known Your beauty and awesomeness
Bring your fire back to those who suffered so terribly they thought You had abandoned them
Help us understand each other and accept each others humanity.

Maker of Miracles, infuse us with the consciousness of a unified world,
A world of realized potentials and true collaborations
A world free of fear, anxiety and insecurity
A world of constant communication between the lower and higher worlds.
Empower us to reveal Your true essence.

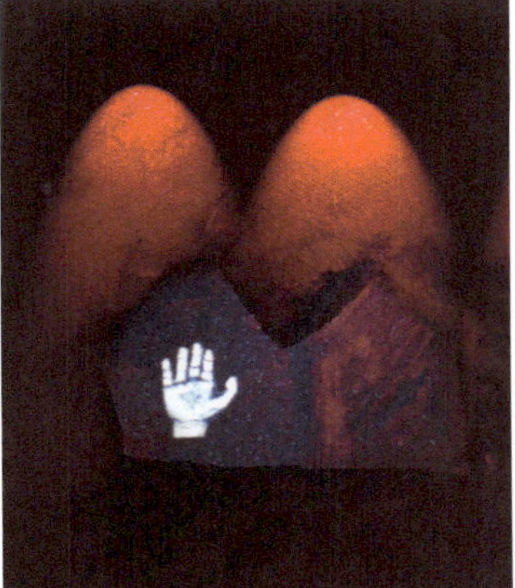

The Foul Smelling Spice

Creo y pido y deseo un buen amor
profundamente tambien deseo
Que me saque las entrañas
Con el que yo tiemble y vuele

No todo tan bonito
lo que huele mal
le da una cierta realidad
profundidad y placer
A la vida.

The foul smelling spice
En el incienso del Templo
Eso es lo que le da el
Último toque

Para que el humo suba
Con fuerza,
Sublime
Real
Intenso y lleno.

La Serena

Si la mar era de leche
Los barquitos de canela
Yo me manchería entera
Por salvar la mi bandiera.

Si la mar era de leche
Yo me haria pexcador
Pexcaría mis dolores
Con palavricas de amor

Si la mar era de leche
Yo me haría vendedor
Caminando y preguntando
¿Dónde se'mpeza l'amor?

En la mar hay una torre
En la torre una ventana
En la ventana una hija
Que a los marineros ama.

Dame la mano tu palomba
Para suvir al tu nido
Maldicha que duermes sola
Vengo a durmir contigo.

No me mates con cuchillo
Ni menos con revolver
Matame con tus amores
En tus brazos muereré.

If the sea were of milk
And boats were of cinnamon
I would stain myself completely
To save my banner.

If the sea were of milk
I would become a fisherman
I would fish out my pain
With words of love.

If the sea were of milk
I would become a salesman
Walking and asking
Where does love begin?

In the sea there's a tower
In the tower there's a window
In the window there's a girl
Who loves sailors.

Give me your hand, dove
So I may come to your nest
Wretched are you that sleeps alone!
I come to sleep with you.

Don't kill me with a knife
Nor with a revolver
Kill me with your love
I will die in your arms.

Midrash of La Serena

This is a modern-day midrash of this famous song of Ladino repertoire, which is reminiscent of the mystic stories of Rebbe Nachman of Breslov. The wonderful Siren in the window, who has the secret to love, is the answer to the concern about woman's alluring danger. She is the soul who is waiting for the seeker to come and experience mystic union.

Midrash is a part of the Oral Torah. This is a midrash of a story with religious significance and gives an explanation of the meanings embedded in the lyrics of *La Serena*. In the tradition of Torah study, ask yourself questions, question the interpretations you find here, see if you can find parallel explanations.

Each of us learns as we question. We must question our assumptions constantly to come to an understanding of our experiences in the world and of the people around us. Every stanza will be interpreted individually, and each reader benefits from the expert advise of the others.

If The Sea Were Made Of Milk

This first stanza of the song creates a beautiful image of a milky sea and boats of cinnamon, a dream understood not only by children but by their parents also. In a perfect world I would be brave and defend truth and right.

If the sea were made of milk. The sea is a representation of the unconscious in nature, the unrevealed, the hidden aspect of reality. Usually it is made of water, which symbolizes Torah, truth and knowledge. Milk symbolizes nurturing and life sustaining love of a mother to its child.

Boats were of cinnamon. Boats are the vessels or containers that float on the great unconscious like Noah's ark, saving us and transporting us to other realms. Cinnamon symbolizes uprightness.

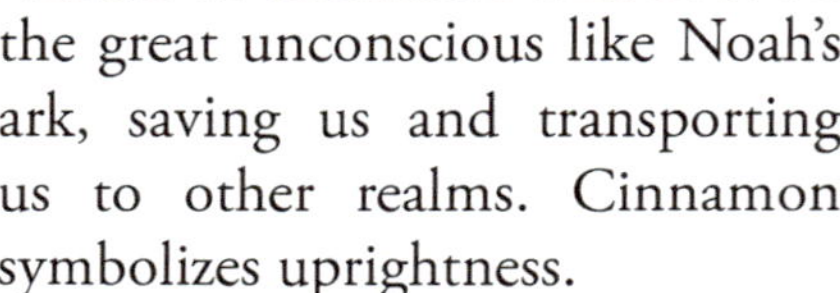

I would stain myself completely. Leave the safety of the vessel and throw myself into the great unconscious, nurturing entity.

To save my banner – For what I believe, my identity, and what defines who I am.

If The Sea Were Made Of Milk

Again we have the imagery of the milky sea. The singer longs to live in that sea with the idea of avoiding pain and finding love.

If the sea were of milk. The unconscious and the nurturing are recurring images like a mantra that carry us through the first part of the song, imagining an ideal world.

I would become a fisherman. The fisherman is he who brings out treasures from the hidden world under the surface of the water. The one who dares venture out beyond the safety of the revealed land into the unknown and brings back sustenance.

I would fish out my pain. What is concealed is the hidden pain of the heart, it takes a risk out into the unknown to "fish it out."

With words of love. The hooks or nets to catch aloof pain are words that show caring, love and compassion.

If The Sea Were Made Of Milk

For the third time, the song makes the same reference, and the singer would become a world traveler dedicated to understanding love and life.

If the sea were made of milk. Now the person is getting to the depth of the issue, first it was identity, second it is to scratch beneath the surface and fish out pain with love, now it is about the origin of love. This is where we start to connect with the Source of All.

I would become a salesman. One who interacts with many people and effects an exchange, either just an exchange of words or one of goods for money.

Walking and asking. Actively searching through the walk and asking those around me, not a passive waiting for the answer to come my way.

Where does love begin? Who is the Source of All? What is the point of beginning of the salve that will heal the pain of my wounds and give me a clear identity?

In The Sea There's A Tower

The soul that learned to long and search for love in the sea identifies the stability and safety of a tower that is the beginning of love.

In the sea there's a tower. Here is a shift in the song, and this gives an answer about where love starts. Now we aren't asking the question so much as trying to understand how to connect with the Source, the place where love starts. The Tower in the Sea represents the body. The Tower symbolizes the body as a recognizable entity that exists within the sea of hidden knowledge, of the unconscious.

In the tower there's a window. The window is the point of transition between the body, the shell that conceals the Source of Love and that Source. The window might be the eye. Eyes are referred to as the windows to the soul. The window could also be the mouth. The mouth is considered to be the point of transition between the body and the soul. It is through speaking and singing that we are able to connect with a person's inner world.

In the window there's a girl. At this point of transition a girl, the soul/*neshama*, waits expectantly, hoping to connect and to answer the earlier question of where love starts.

Who loves sailors. The sailor is the seeker. The girl, the *neshama*, loves those who seek her out to connect with her and she peers out of the window in her tower waiting for the one who will come looking for her.

Give Me Your Hand, Dove

In this stanza something new happens. In the tower in the middle of the milky sea, the singer has found love and satisfaction in life. The dream of the traveler upon the sea is to have the comfort of home and not sleeping alone

Give me your hand, dove. Help me reach you, by giving me a hand. Make for me a point of connection, oh dove/soul. The dove (*paloma*) is a symbol for the soul and for Israel that goes as far back as the poetry of Yehuda HaLevi in the middle ages. The dove, being a bird of peace, has an element of transcendence because it flies away from our world, the world of land/manifestation.

So I may come to your nest. If you facilitate my reaching you then I can come to where you dwell. The nest is also a symbol for the place where the Messiah (*Moshiah*) awaits his coming. It is a place of unfulfilled potential, an incubator of sorts where potential is developing until the time it is ripe to manifest in the physical world.

Wretched are you that sleeps alone! How unfortunate, oh dove, oh *neshama*, oh girl, oh soul that you are alone and I had not connected with you before. You must have endured years of loneliness and wondered if I would never come seeking you.

I come to sleep with you. Now I am ready for the connection that you deserve and that you seek. I am coming to your nest, the chamber of my developing potential and sleeping with you so we may connect on the deepest levels available.

Don't Kill Me With A Knife

This dramatic plea is for the ultimate union through sweetness.

Don't kill me with a knife. My transformation should not come in a searing realization, like the blade of a knife that cuts through what is.

Nor with a revolver. My transformation should not come through fire, like the gunpowder of a bullet that consumes what it penetrates.

Kill me with your love. My transformation, death (mystical ecstasy) should come only through your love. I want to reach the level of losing my very life in the transformation that will take place when we are intimate.

I will die in your arms. This connection will make me transcend the previous life that I knew. In your embrace, in your sexual, mystical ecstasy embrace, I will transform into the new me, discard my old self and become the new self you lead me towards.

Conclusions on La Serena

This entire song refers to our spiritual awakening and the different stages through which we must pass to reach a point of spiritual transformation that culminates in mystical ecstasy. First there is a search for identity, then a confrontation of pain, finally a question of what is the Source of love. At this point the realization of the soul comes in to the song and the desire to connect with the soul, a sadness of the time lost and the excitement of finally consummating the connection. In the final stanza the seeker requests for this awakening to come through sweetness and love and not painful experiences.

Concluding Thoughts

In Judaism fish are symbols of fertility. During the New Year (*Rosh Hashana*) sins are cast away into a body of water containing fish so they can carry the sins away to the sea. Fish are suitable for this task because their eyes are always open. Since they have ever open eyes and are covered by water they are not subject to the evil eye. Fish are the only animals that were not affected by the flood. They have a primordial connection to the original Creation.

Sirens connect women to this fish quality of protection from the evil eye. As the ones who bear children, women also have a connection to primordial creation. The womb, the mikveh, and the sea all have similar elements.

Sirens were originally bird-women. That is, they had wings. The Cherubs (*kruvim*) that hovered in marital embrace over the ark in the Holy of Holies also have wings. Rabbi Ginsburgh teaches that a woman's voice comes from that most intimate point between the Cherubs in the Holy of Holies. In other words, from the most intimate place of the most intimate chamber in the entire Creation.

The ultimate female voice is one that penetrates reality by connecting the holy (*kodesh*) to the mundane (*chol*). The power of one's voice determines one's ability to unite the Holy and the Mundane in an effective way. In fact, the Zohar says there's a voice

that has the power to resurrect the dead. Anything can be turned from the furthest extent of impurity to the highest level of purity.

This is woman's song. It can have the fallen, blemished aspect of alluring, beguiling and mortal danger. However, we will only know that redemption is afoot when the woman's voice is getting stronger and stronger. Women's holy and rectified song is the herald of Messianic times. It is the song of the wondrous voice that comes from the chamber where the Messiah is waiting, a bird's nest.

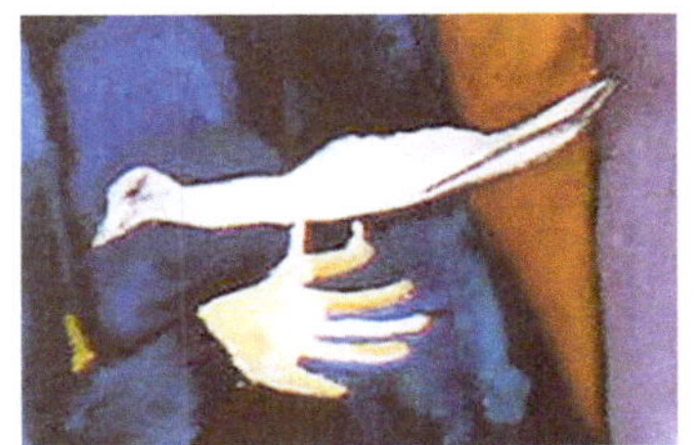

Glossary

Flor de Serena – It means "Siren's Flower", and it is a music group based in Los Angeles that is dedicated to the performance of Sephardic music in Ladino (Judeo-Spanish language).

Hod she'be Malchut – *Hod* means "splendor", and *Malchut* means the "kingdom". Both are important *sefirot* in Kabalah, points in the body of special significance.

Kabbalah – The Jewish mystical tradition. The simple meaning of the word Kabbalah means "to receive." It has another meaning, that of parallels. A Kabbalist finds parallels that elucidate an added meaning about something's essence. For example in regards to gematria (numerology): The word *Amalek* (the Archenemy of the Jewish people who is always out to destroy us in each generation) has the same numerology as *Safek*, the word for doubt. Doubt is our archenemy and can destroy us. Hebrew letters each stand for a number. Every word has its numerology. We can understand the inner workings of Creation when we familiarize ourselves with these parallels that are hidden within each word.

Kol Isha – Hebrew for "the woman's voice". It refers to the Jewish law that men should not hear the voice of a woman in song because it would be too enticing for them and might lead to inappropriate thoughts.

Ladina – A Portuguese based registered non-profit society dedicated to rescuing the memory and culture of the Portuguese Jewish people.

Notzer Hesed – This refers to the kindness of Hashem, which extends not only to us but to all past and future generations.

Omer – The barley offering brought to the Temple from the second day of Passover until the day before Shavuot. Today, we count these days one by one. There are seven weeks and the counting totals to 49 days. The 50th day is the holiday of Shavuot (weeks), which celebrates the giving of the Torah on Mount Sinai. Each of the seven weeks represents one of the seven lower sefirot inter-included with each other. This is a process of spiritual refinement that is supposed to bring us to a higher level of development so as to be ready to receive the Torah anew on Shavuot.

Palácio Das Sereias – In English Palace of the Sirens. It stands on top of a hill in the city of Porto, Portugal. Its distinctive feature are two large mermaids carved in stone on either side of the entrance. It is now a home for aging nuns.

Tzinorot – Channels through which Divine blessing flows into the physical world.

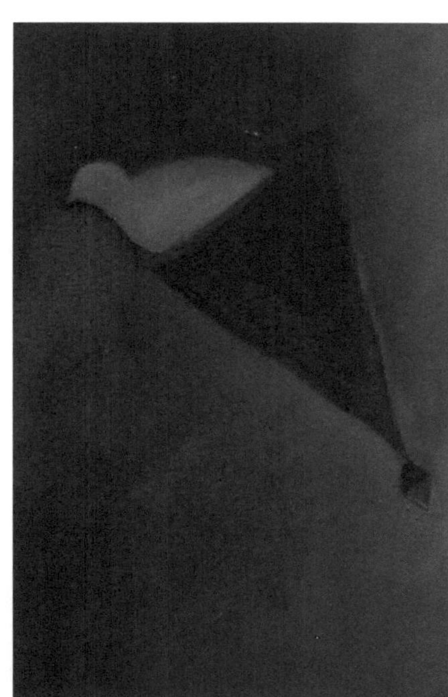

Suggested Readings

***Kabbalah** (Jewish mysticism)*:

Frankiel, Tamar
The Gift of Kabbalah: Discovering the Secrets of Heaven, Renewing Your Life on Earth. Jewish Lights Publishing. 2001.

Ginsburgh, Rabbi Yitzak
•*Living in Divine Space: Kabbalah and Meditation*. Gal Einai. 2003.
•*Awakening the Spark Within: Five Dynamics of Leadership That Can Change the World.* Gal Einai. 2001.
•*The Hebrew Letters: Channels of Creative Consciousness.* Gal Einai. 1995.

Glazerson, Rabbi M.
Music and Kabbalah. Yerid HaSefarim. 1988.

Pinson, DovBer
Inner Rhythms: The Kabbalah of Music. Jason Aronson. 1999.

Matt, Daniel C.
The Essential Kabbalah: The Heart of Jewish Mysticism. HarperCollins. 1995.

Greenbaum, Avraham, Compiler and translator
Rabbi Nachman's Tikkun. Breslov Research Institute. 1984.

Luzzato, Rabbi Moshe Chaim
138 Openings of Wisdom. Translated by Avraham Greenbaum. Azamra Institute. 2005.

Schwarz, Arturo
Kabbalah and Alchemy: An Essay on Common Archetypes. Jason Aronson Inc. 2000.

***Mussar** (Jewish self-improvement)*:

Cordovero, Rabbi Moshe
The Palm Tree of Devorah. Originally published in the 16th century. Targum Press. 1993.

Finkelman, Rabbi Shimon and Rabbi Yitzhak Berkowitz
Chofetz Chaim A Lesson a Day: The Concepts and Laws of Proper Speech arranged for Daily Study. Mesorah Publications. 2001.

Goldberger, Moshe
Master Your Thoughts: Discover and Use your Inner Guide. Targum/Feldheim. 2000.

Luzzato, Rabbi Moshe Chaim
Mesilot Yesharim: The Path of the Just. Originally published in the 18th century. Feldheim. 2004.

Satanov, Rabbi Mendel of
Cheshbon Ha-Nefesh. Originally published in 1845. Feldheim Publishers. 1995.

Jewish Women:

Elper, Ora Wiskind and Susan Handelman, editors
Torah of the Mothers: Contemporary Jewish Women Read Classical Jewish Texts. Urim Publications. 2006.

Frankiel, Tamar
The Voice of Sarah: Femenine Spirituality and Traditional Judaism. Biblio Press. 1990.

Shlit'a. Megama, The Biala Rebbe
Mevaser Tov: The Merit of the Righteous Women. Ginzei Maharitz Institute. 2003.

Meditation, Prophecy, Advice:

Breslov, Rabbi Nathan of
Advice (Likutey Etzot). Translated by Avraham Greenbaum. Breslov Research Institute. 1983.

Kaplan, Aryeh
Meditation and the Bible. Samuel Weiser, Inc. 1978.

Naor, Bezalel
Lights of Prophecy. Orthodox Union. 1990.

Other Traditions:

Khan, Hazrat Inayat
The Mysticism of Sound and Music: The Sufi Teachings of Hazrat Inayat Khan. Shambhala Publications, 1991.

Campbell, Joseph with Bill Moyers
The Power of Myth. Doubleday. 1988.

www.ingramcontent.com/pod-product-compliance
Lightning Source LLC
LaVergne TN
LVHW070140110826
845147LV00002B/296

9780977751457